Where Slow Food and Whole Food Meet

Where Slow Food and Whole Food Meet:

healthy slow cooker dinners from our kitchens to yours

edited by: Jennifer Dempsey
Christine Pittman

To all of our amazing readers from around the world, thank you for joining us on our culinary adventures and for letting us bring our recipes and stories from our kitchens into yours.

Contents

Welcome to our Kitchens

When we teamed up to create this cookbook as a fundraising tool for food banks across the United States, our goal was to have a beautiful book full of healthy delicious recipes that would fit easily into everyday life. We did it!

Over thirty amazing food bloggers have contributed nutritious recipes and stunning food photography to fill these pages. Their recipes are all as healthy and fresh as we'd hoped. When you cook from this book you'll know that your family is getting the nutrients they need.

Our purpose for creating this book was so that food banks across the United States could use it to increase donations during Hunger Action Month, September 2014. We therefore wanted the recipes to be affordable as well as healthy and delicious. The contributing bloggers did a great job with this and most of the recipes in the book are under $3.00 per serving. Whether you're new to slow cooking or have used your beloved slow cooker for years, the affordability of these recipes probably isn't a surprise to you; the brilliant thing about using a slow cooker is that it turns more humble meats, legumes and vegetables into mouthwatering meals. And that's what you'll find in this book: Mouthwatering meals that are healthy, affordable and easy to make. Recipes that we know your family will love as much as ours do.

If you like the recipes in this book, please find us, the food bloggers who contributed recipes to the book, online and in social media so that you can see more of the delicious dishes coming out of our kitchens. We look forward to hearing your feedback and to continuing the conversation about slow cooking and healthy low-cost meals.

From our kitchens to yours,
Christine, Jennifer and Our Fellow Food Blogging Contributors

Incorporating Whole Foods into Quick & Easy Slow Cooker Meals

When most people think of cooking in their slow cookers, they think of meat. Things like Pot Roast and Pulled Pork. While it's true that slow cookers love these big cuts of meat, slow cooking is also a friend to other whole ingredients like vegetables, legumes, grains and dairy products.

Extra Vegetables

One way to quickly and easily incorporate healthy ingredients into your slow cooker meals is to add them to your old standby recipes. Making a pot roast? Throw in carrots, potatoes and onions. Pulled pork in the pot? Add some chopped tomatoes and bell peppers. Anytime you have meat in the slow cooker you can add fresh or frozen vegetables to increase the nutrients in the meal. Try these recipes for a veggie boost to your meaty plate.

Whole Tuscan Chicken - page 27
Chicken and Sausage Gumbo - page 35
Chicken Cacciatore - page 43

Slow-Cooking Legumes

Legumes are simple to add to slow cooker recipes. Dried legumes like chickpeas, split peas and kidney beans are inexpensive and yet so full of the nutrients that our bodies need. The usual drawback to dried legumes is that they take a long time to cook but when you're using a slow cooker that becomes an advantage. Long and slow cooking is perfect for legumes. Add them to any long-cooking slow cooker meal, making sure to add liquid, and they will cook slowly along with the other ingredients. Try these recipes to learn the technique of cooking legumes in the slow cooker.

Harvest Chili - page 62
Lentil, Sausage and Kale Stew - page 70
Cuban Black Bean Soup - page 87

Experimenting with Grains

Grains can be tricky in the slow cooker. The worry is that the long cooking will lead to a mushy texture. To avoid mushiness we often cook grains like rice separately and serve them as a side dish to our slow cooker meals. But if you want to try it out, we have some advice.

Add quick-cooking grains like rice, pasta, quinoa and couscous the last hour or so of cooking, making sure that there's a nice amount of liquid in the slow cooker before you add the grain. Sturdier longer-cooking grains like barley and farro can be added at the beginning of the recipe. Here are examples of recipes that incorporate grain and pasta into the slow cooker so that you can see how it's done.

Chicken, Potato and Barley Stew - page 73
Lasagna - page 40

Adding Dairy

If you're thinking of adding dairy products to the slow cooker we advise working cautiously. When cooked for a long time, dairy products can separate and curdle. If this happens, don't worry. The food is still safe and edible. It just looks strange. Here are four tips that can help prevent curdling.

First, use higher fat dairy items. This means choosing whole milk or cream instead of fat-free milk because the higher fat content can insulate the proteins against curdling. Second, if you're going to have dairy in your slow cooker, don't add acidic ingredients like tomato, vinegar or citrus juice. The higher acidity in the liquid can cause the proteins in the dairy to clump up and curdle. Third, if there's dairy in the recipe use the low setting to cook the meal. This keeps the slow cooker at a lower temperature than that at which curdling usually occurs. The final and safest anti-curdling tip is to consider adding the dairy at the end of the cooking process after you have turned off the slow cooker. This way your dairy is not being heated much and won't reach a temperature that can lead to curdling. Here are two recipes for you to try that add dairy at the end of the cooking process.

Creamy Chicken and Veggies - page 24
Chicken Korma - page 92

We hope that the above tips help you add healthy whole ingredients to your slow cooking repertoire and that you and your family love the results.

Slow Cooker Tips for Busy Families

The beauty of slow cooking is that you can quickly prepare a meal and then move on with your day while the slow cooker cooks for you. But knowing the techniques that lead to delicious slow cooker meals is essential for success. Here are some tips from contributing bloggers to help you get started.

Choosing the Right Meat

Choose tougher cuts over leaner cuts of meat. Tougher cuts have more fat which helps keep the meat juicy and they have more connective tissue which breaks down and leads to tenderness. Without that fat or connective tissue, lean cuts can end up stringy and dry. Choose well-marbled stewing-style beef and pot roasts over grilling steaks, choose pork butt and shoulder over loin and choose chicken thighs or drumsticks over breasts. Bonus, these tough cuts are often the cheapest! -Jennifer Dempsey of Mother Thyme

No Chicken Skin, Please

Don't leave the skin on chicken. It ends up flaccid and rubbery and not at all good unless you grill or broil it after slow cooking, which is a cool technique to try. -Christine Pittman of Cook the Story

Brown It

You should always brown ground meat and then drain off the fat before adding it to the slow cooker. Otherwise you'll be cooking in a pool of grease and your meat will have a mealy texture. -Jennifer Dempsey of Mother Thyme

Prep Ahead

Chop vegetables and cook meat the night before for a quick morning slow cooker routine. Just be sure to store them separately in the fridge until you're ready to get cooking. -Nicole from Wonky Wonderful

Extra Flavor

Browning chunks of meat and larger roasts before slow cooking is optional but may be worth the few minutes since it adds a rich flavor to the dish. Deglaze the skillet with water or another liquid after browning the meat and add that in for even more flavor. -Jennifer Dempsey of Mother Thyme

Defrost First

Never cook frozen meat in your slow cooker. Slow cookers don't reliably get frozen meat up to a safe temperature (above 140°F) evenly enough or quickly enough. Your meat will likely spend too much time in the danger zone (from 40°F - 140°F), which can allow bacteria to flourish. Instead, thaw your meat over a day or two in the refrigerator. Or, use your microwave's defrost setting to gently thaw your meat (checking often and rotating it to avoid cooking some parts while others remain frozen), then immediately transfer it into your slow cooker to get it cooking and rapidly up to a safe temperature. -Gretchen Fritsch and Shelley Fulton of Two Healthy Kitchens

When to Taste
Taste your slow cooker meal an hour before cooking is complete. Add salt, pepper and spices as needed so that they can penetrate the dish in the final hour. -Nicole from Wonky Wonderful

How Full Is Too Full?
For food to cook evenly, don't fill your slow cooker more than ⅔ full. -Jennifer Dempsey of Mother Thyme

Less Liquid
One thing that surprises people when they first use a slow cooker is how much liquid can end up in the pot at the end. The slow cooking process extracts a lot of juices from meats and other foods. Therefore, when you start improvising recipes with your slow cooker, it's important to add liquid sparingly or you'll have more than expected at the end. -Christine Pittman of Cook the Story

No peeking!
Once you turn your slow cooker on, don't keep opening the lid and checking it. The beauty of the slow cooker is that you can turn it on and walk away! If you take off the lid it lets heat out and disrupts the cooking process and your food will take longer to cook. -Taylor from Food Faith Fitness

Spice it up
It's best to add dry herbs at the beginning of cooking and save fresh herbs for the end. Fresh herbs have a more subtle flavor that will be lost in the long cooking process. They will also turn brown and ugly after the hours of warming. -Jennifer Dempsey of Mother Thyme

Get Used to It
One tricky thing about slow cookers is that they're not all the same. They come in different sizes and they can heat at slightly different temperatures. And definitely, slow cookers from decades ago didn't cook at the same temperatures that slow cookers do today. These factors can affect how long a recipe needs to cook. I use the amount of time given in slow cooker recipes as a guide. I then rely on my own experience with my own slow cooker. This comes with practice and from using the slow cooker often. -Christine Pittman from Cook the Story

Affordable Cooking

As we began collaborating on *Where Whole Food and Slow Food Meet* we knew that we wanted this book to benefit food banks because slow cooking is so cost effective. It was a natural fit.

All the proceeds from the print version of this book are going to the *Second Harvest Food Bank of Central Florida*. In addition, numerous food banks across the country are using the ebook version of this cookbook as an incentive to encourage people to donate during Hunger Action Month, September 2014.

We hope that this book will be cherished by those of you who love slow cooking but that it will also be a resource for those who struggle with hunger. We have therefore included a price-per-serving amount with each recipe. You will see that most of the recipes in this book are under $3.00 per serving (costs calculated at a single mid-range grocery store in Central Florida in August 2014). We hope that this information will be helpful when you're deciding what to cook for your family.

Price-Per-Serving and Actual Cost

As we were calculating the price-per-serving for the recipes, we quickly realized that price-per-serving doesn't always equate with actual cost. While the low price-per-serving figures in this book are accurate, they don't necessarily reflect what a shopper needs to put into their grocery cart to make the recipe. This happens whenever required ingredients are only partially used in a recipe.

For example, the *Butternut Squash Vegetarian Chili* on page 58 calls for 1 cup of frozen corn. We calculated the price-per-serving by taking the cost of a full bag of frozen corn ($2.92) and dividing it by the number of cups it contains (6½). This yields the price of $0.45 which goes into the price-per-serving calculations. However, if a grocery-shopper doesn't have a bag of corn in their freezer at home, they need to buy the larger $2.92 bag. In that case, the amount they need to actually spend is more than what the price-per-serving listed on the recipe would lead them to expect.

When the issue is one bag of corn, this may not result in a large discrepancy. But if a recipe calls for olive oil and you don't already have some, the difference would be greater since a bottle of olive oil can be very expensive. If you buy several ingredients that will only be partially used, a seemingly inexpensive recipe can become very costly in real terms.

In recognition of this disparity we have some ideas to help keep the recipes in this book, and all recipes that you attempt, more affordable.

Stocking Up On Pantry Staples

Most of the items that are partially used in a recipe fall under the category of *Pantry Staples*. These are things like oils, vinegars, spices, rice, grains, and canned goods. Having a well-stocked pantry will help keep recipe costs down. Unfortunately, attaining a well-stocked pantry is an expensive prospect. A more affordable way to get there is to do it gradually.

Find a recipe that calls for 1 or 2 staples that you don't already have. Add that recipe to your meal plan for the week and put the new staples on your list. If you include 1 or 2 new staples every week, you won't need to spend a great deal extra at one time and will slowly find that you have more items on hand with which to make meals.

Making the same recipe again a couple of weeks later will ensure that you use the staples and get value out of them. Or, you can look for other recipes that use the same ingredients.

Maintaining Your Pantry

Once you have a stash of pantry items, create a *Running Low List* to put alongside your regular grocery list. Add pantry items to this list before they run out so that you don't have to buy them immediately. Instead, you'll have the freedom to watch for sales and coupons. When a "Buy One, Get One Free" or other sale happens on an item from your Running Low List, buy it if you can. This is particularly useful when thinking about expensive pantry items like olive oil and some spices. Even for less expensive items, the savings add up over time.

Multi-Purposing Produce

When it comes to fresh produce, which is featured heavily in this book, a similar problem can arise where the fruits or vegetables are pre-packaged in a larger amount than what you require for the recipe. In this situation, the best strategy is to plan another recipe for later in the week that uses the same produce.

It is also possible to make the same recipe but to switch a few things to make it different. For instance, if you buy a big bag of kale to make the *Lentil, Sausage and Kale Stew* on page 70, you can change a few ingredients to create a whole new dish another night. Swap out the lentils for cannellini beans, change the seasonings from Herbs de Provence to a dry Italian seasoning blend and add some canned diced tomatoes. Serve it over pasta and you have a completely different dish that uses the same fresh produce that you had already purchased.

You can also purchase produce when it's in season and then freeze it to use when it costs more. Wash and chop items before you freeze them so they can be conveniently added to recipes. Freezing works for vegetables like peppers and tomatoes, which can be handy to throw into fall and winter soups and stews, and also for fruits like blueberries, strawberries and peaches. Stock up when they're in peak (and cheap) season and then enjoy them throughout the winter in smoothies, oatmeal and desserts.

Managing Meat

The fact that meat adds a lot to the cost of meals was reinforced for us again and again as we calculated the price-per-servings for this book. It is therefore a good idea to have a plan to save money on your meat purchases.

Purchase meat like chicken breast when it's on sale or buy it in bulk. Stores vary on their family bulk pricing but you can often find chicken breast for as little as $1.99 per pound. Package the bulk meat into 1 pound bags and freeze. You will be amazed at the savings, especially when you consider that chicken breast can cost as much as $4 per pound when it's not sold in bulk. Buying in bulk costs more at the outset, but you save in the long run. This is true for other types of meat as well. Buy all types of meat in bulk or when they're on sale and then freeze in smaller portions.

As with the pantry staples above, you can also build your frozen meat inventory slowly. Buy something at a good price whenever you can and then package it and freeze it. You might buy chicken breasts one week and ground beef the next. Slowly you will end up with a variety of frozen meats on hand. Once you have a selection in your freezer, you can start adding meats to your Running Low List so that you remember to buy it when it's on sale.

As your inventory grows, make sure to remember what you have in the freezer. Label everything with the date and with what it is (a sharpie marker works perfectly on freezer bags). Create a list of everything you've put in your freezer and cross things off as you use them. This makes it easier to plan meals because you'll know what you already have. It will also help you use up the items in your freezer.

Meal Planning

Meal planning is one way to cook more affordably. It requires a little time when you first start, but it gets easier as you get used to it. One tip to speed things up is to keep your meal plans from weeks past. You can reuse them again and again when you don't have time to create a new one, no effort required.

Make your meal plan by first assessing what you have on hand. Look to your freezer list and your pantry staples to see what you already have. Then create meal ideas using those items. Second, look at what's on sale at your local grocery store. Create a menu with items that you can get on sale. Combining sale items with coupons is an additional way to save. Look online for printable coupons, and look over your weekly grocery store ads to combine store savings with coupons. There are blogs, websites and forums that will even break down local grocery store savings and coupons to maximize your savings.

When creating a meal plan it's easiest to have a starting place. Consider keeping a list of your family's favorite meals to glance at as you make your plan. You can even store those recipes in a binder so they're easy to find when it's time to cook. In your repertoire, be sure to include several meatless dinners that use mostly pantry staples like dried legumes and canned tomatoes. This can be a big help on days when you're running low on food and can't go to the grocery store. Once you have your meal plan in place, consult it to make a grocery list. Go to the store armed with your list, coupons and the store ads. And then, stick to your list.

Grocery Shopping Tips

When at the grocery store it's important to keep track of what's going into your cart. Use a calculator to tally your spending as you shop.

Try to stick to your grocery list. If you spot something that you want but that isn't on your list, put it in the top of the shopping cart basket. Add all unlisted items there. If you have money left over when you've completed your shopping, decide if you want or need the items from the top of your cart.

In general, cooking affordably comes down to planning. From gradually stocking your pantry and freezer, to making a meal plan and deciding how you will grocery shop. Everything involves having a plan and sticking to it.

We know planning can be tough for a variety of reasons. If you're in a situation where you can make plans and follow through most of the time, that will be your best strategy. If it's more difficult to plan ahead, doing so whenever possible will still help and will make a difference to your family's food cost.

In a nation so abundant in food resources, it is profoundly tragic that more than 40 million of our American neighbors cannot afford enough of this basic resource each year. Feeding America network food banks across this country help to anchor an important safety net of more than 50,000 nonprofit feeding programs by providing nearly 3 billion pounds of groceries annually for children, seniors, working poor families, homeless, and others in need. Sadly, even this incredible outreach is not enough...much more work remains to be accomplished in order that everyone who needs help with food can get it. Feeding America food banks work diligently every day to grow their missions into that gap of need, and to stretch toward the day when all the cups, bowls, and plates of our nation can be filled. And when those who are struggling can be filled with hope for their futures.

-Second Harvest Food Bank of Central Florida

CHICKEN DINNERS

Creamy Chicken and Veggies
Whole Tuscan Chicken
Chicken with 40 Cloves of Garlic
Creamy Buffalo Chicken
Mango Chicken
Chicken and Sausage Gumbo
Autumn Apple Chicken Sandwiches

Creamy Chicken and Veggies

Christine Pittman of Cook the Story

For this easy chicken dinner, broccoli, cauliflower and lemon slices sit over chicken pieces and soak up flavor as they steam. Once everything is cooked, the juices from the chicken and vegetables are mixed with cream cheese and lemon juice to make a luscious sauce. Serve with egg noodles or on a bed of rice.

1 teaspoon olive oil
6 boneless, skinless chicken thighs (about 1½-2 pounds)
¼ teaspoon salt
¼ teaspoon black pepper
1 pound cauliflower florets
1 pound broccoli florets
1 teaspoon oregano
½ teaspoon garlic powder
1 lemon, in ¼ inch slices
4 ounces cream cheese
1 teaspoon lemon juice
Freshly chopped parsley for garnish (optional)

Rub the olive oil around the bottom and up the sides of a slow cooker. Add the chicken in a single layer. Sprinkle with the salt and pepper. Top with the cauliflower and broccoli florets. Sprinkle with the oregano and garlic powder. Arrange the lemon slices in a single layer over top.

Cook until chicken is cooked through, 2-3 hours on high, 4-6 hours on low.

Use tongs to remove lemon slices. Discard. Transfer cauliflower and broccoli to a serving plate. Top with the chicken pieces. Strain any juices that remain into a measuring cup.

Put the cream cheese in a microwave-safe bowl and microwave until very soft, 30-45 seconds. Add ¼ cup of the strained juices. Stir until smooth. Stir in the lemon juice. Season with salt and pepper to taste, if desired. Drizzle cream cheese sauce over chicken and vegetables.

Serves 4   *$3.48 per serving*

Whole Tuscan Chicken
by Julie Deily of The Little Kitchen

An Italian variation of a very popular recipe on my blog The Little Kitchen, this meal is super-quick to put together. Since you broil the chicken after it's done cooking in the slow cooker, it will be like you roasted a whole chicken, Tuscan-style!

3 teaspoons salt
2 teaspoons paprika
1½ teaspoons dried thyme
½ teaspoon garlic salt
½ teaspoon dried rosemary
¼ teaspoon dried oregano
¼ teaspoon ground black pepper
1 lemon, juiced and zested
8 cloves garlic, minced, divided
1½ pounds small red potatoes, larger ones halved or quartered
1 onion, chopped
3 carrots, cut in half lengthwise and then into quarters
1½ tablespoons olive oil, divided
3½ to 4½ pounds whole roasting or fryer chicken
1 lemon, quartered

Put salt, paprika, thyme, garlic salt, rosemary, oregano and black pepper in a small bowl and mix together. Set aside. Add the lemon zest and half of the minced garlic cloves to the bowl of seasonings and mix again.

Add the potatoes, onions and carrots to the bottom of the slow cooker. Pour lemon juice and 1 tablespoon of the olive oil on top the vegetables and mix to coat. Add the other half of the minced garlic cloves on top of the vegetables.

Wipe the chicken dry with a paper towel. Fold the wings down. Separate the skin from the breast and drumsticks with your fingers, but be careful not to rip the skin. Place some of the seasonings under the skin.

Rub chicken with ½ tablespoon olive oil. Add the seasoning inside and all over the chicken. Add quartered lemons to the inside of the chicken. Tie the legs together with kitchen twine. Place the chicken on top of the vegetables inside the slow cooker.

Cook on high for 4 to 6 hours or on low for 6 to 9 hours. (Cook until the internal temperature of the leg is at 160 degrees F.)

Remove the chicken using turkey lifters and place in a roasting pan or oven-safe glass dish. Broil in your oven at 550 degrees F (or the highest your oven broiler will go) for 5 to 10 minutes. (Be careful and watch it to ensure it doesn't burn.) Serve chicken with vegetables from the slow cooker.

Serves 6-8   *$1.98 per serving*

Chicken with 40 Cloves of Garlic
by Wendy O'Neal of Around My Family Table

Don't be scared by all the garlic, the slow cooking method mellows out the intense garlic flavor and makes this chicken tender and full of earthy flavors. Perfect comfort food any time of the year!

10-12 chicken legs
40 cloves garlic, peeled
1 small onion, thinly sliced
2 tablespoons fresh lemon juice, plus the leftover lemon wedges
4 sprigs thyme
2 bay leaves
2 teaspoons paprika
Salt and pepper

Lightly grease the inside of your slow cooker with oil or no-stick cooking spray. Add half of the onions and ⅓ of the garlic cloves to the bottom of the pot.

Season chicken legs with salt, pepper, and paprika. Place half the legs in the slow cooker over garlic and onions. Add 2 sprigs of thyme and both bay leaves. Layer the remaining onion and another ⅓ of the garlic cloves. Top with remaining chicken legs and finally the rest of the garlic and thyme.

Drizzle the lemon juice over the chicken and add the squeezed lemon pieces to the pot. Cover and cook on low for 6-8 hours.

Optional: When chicken is cooked, remove liquid and place in a small pot on the stove. Combine 1 tablespoon cornstarch to ¼ cup water and add to the chicken broth. Let the sauce thicken and serve over the top of the chicken.

Notes: Buy pre-peeled garlic for quick and easy prep. If you prefer, lightly brown chicken legs on the stove over medium-high heat with 1 tablespoon extra virgin olive oil before adding to the stoneware for cooking.

Serves 6 $2.15 per serving

Creamy Buffalo Chicken
by Jennifer Dempsey of Mother Thyme

Everything you love about Buffalo Chicken mixed into one delicious slow cooker meal. Loaded with baby carrots, celery and onion, this will quickly become a family favorite. Great for a busy weeknight or serve it at your next football party. Enjoy over rice or even egg noodles.

2 pounds boneless, skinless chicken breast, cut into large bite size pieces
½ teaspoon salt
Pinch of black pepper
½ cup Buffalo wing sauce
½ cup chicken broth
1 cup baby carrots, cut in half or thirds
½ cup chopped sweet onion
½ cup chopped celery (about 2 ribs)
¼ cup all-purpose flour
3-4 tablespoons water
1 (8 ounce) package cream cheese, softened
¼ teaspoon dried parsley flakes
¼ teaspoon dried dill
¼ teaspoon garlic powder
⅛ teaspoon onion powder
Cooked rice or egg noodles for serving

Season chicken with salt and pepper and place in slow cooker. Stir in wing sauce and chicken broth. Top with carrots, onion and celery. Cover and cook on low for about 6 hours, or until chicken is cooked through.

In a small bowl mix flour with the water until flour is dissolved. Stir into slow cooker and cook for another 15 minutes until sauce thickens.

In a small bowl mix cream cheese with parsley, dill, garlic powder and onion powder. Stir into slow cooker, then turn off heat.

Serve over rice or egg noodles.

Serves 4-6   *$4.19 per serving*

Mango Chicken
by Megan Myers of Stetted

This recipe is inspired by the bold flavors of Indian cooking, but is mild enough for the whole family to enjoy. Garam masala is a spice blend that now is available in most grocery stores. Any variety of mango can be used, and feel free to swap in the more economical frozen mango, if you like.

1 pound boneless, skinless chicken thighs
Salt and pepper
1 pound sweet potato, cubed
1 cup diced yellow onion
1 (15 ounce) can diced tomatoes
1 cup coconut milk
1 cup chicken stock
1 tablespoon garam masala
1½ cups diced mango
Cooked rice for serving (optional)

Turn the slow cooker on low.

Place chicken thighs in the slow cooker and sprinkle with a pinch of salt and pepper. Add remaining ingredients and cover slow cooker.

Cook on low for 6 hours, or until chicken is cooked through. Shred chicken into smaller chunks. Stir and season with salt and pepper to taste. Serve over cooked rice if desired.

Serves 4-6

$2.44 per serving

Chicken and Sausage Gumbo
by Morgan Perkins of Peaches Please

Summer is a great time for fresh produce and one of my favorite Southern veggies is okra. Fresh okra is like garden candy. While I love eating okra sautéed lightly with a little olive oil and salt, gumbo is probably the most iconic okra dish. The okra acts as a natural thickener, adding body and flavor to the dish. The spiciness and availability of fresh okra makes gumbo a natural fit for summer, but it also makes for a hearty cold weather supper, served over hot rice and alongside a helping of fresh cornbread.

8 chicken thighs
6 sausages, andouille or Italian
½ cup flour
3 cups chicken stock
26 ounces canned or boxed chopped tomatoes
1 yellow onion, diced
5 celery ribs, chopped
1 green bell pepper, diced
1 red bell pepper, diced
4 cloves garlic, minced
1½ teaspoons dried oregano
1½ teaspoons dried thyme
1½ teaspoons smoked paprika
1 teaspoon salt
¾ teaspoons cayenne pepper
¼ teaspoon black pepper
3 cups chopped fresh okra, stem ends discarded (frozen can be used in lieu of fresh, if fresh is unavailable)

Place the chicken thighs skin side down in a room temperature frying pan and then heat the pan to med-high, rendering the fat out of the skin. Flip the chicken thighs to brown the other side and remove the skin from the thighs. Discard the skin. Flip the chicken again to brown the first, now skinless, side. Remove the chicken thighs from the pan and set them in the slow cooker.

Brown the sausages in the pan, then cut the sausages into pieces and add them to the slow cooker. Turn the heat down to low and sprinkle the flour into the rendered fat in the pan, whisking to fully incorporate the flour and create a roux. Gently cook the roux at a bare simmer for about 20 minutes, stirring frequently, until the roux is approximately the color of peanut butter. Scrape the roux into the slow cooker.

Add the following ingredients to the slow cooker: chicken stock, chopped tomatoes, onion, celery, green bell pepper, red bell pepper, garlic, oregano, thyme, paprika, salt, cayenne and black pepper. Give the slow cooker a brief stir, cover and cook on low for 6 hours.

At the 6 hour mark, add the okra and turn the heat to high. Cook on high for 2 hours. Once the gumbo has finished cooking, skin the accumulated oil off of the top and serve the gumbo spooned over rice.

Serves 8-10

$3.44 per serving

Autumn Apple Chicken Sandwiches

by Caroline Edwards of Chocolate & Carrots

An Autumn inspired pulled chicken sandwich recipe with hints of curry and cinnamon! This chicken is great served on buns with apple slices and fresh spinach leaves.

2 pounds boneless, skinless chicken breasts
3 granny smith apples, peeled, cored and diced
2 medium sweet onions, diced
½ cup dried cranberries
½ cup stock or water
1 teaspoon curry powder
½ teaspoon cinnamon
Salt and pepper, to taste

Place all ingredients in a slow cooker and stir together. Cook on low for 6 hours.

Take the chicken breasts out then shred them with 2 forks and stir back into the slow cooker.

Serves 6-8 people   *$2.48 per serving*

VIVA ITALIA!

Lasagna
Chicken Cacciatore
Pork Tenderloin Florentine
Italian Beef Sandwiches
Balsamic Orange Roast Beef
Sweet Italian Sausage and Peppers
Macaroni and Cheese with Sugar Snap Peas
Pork Meatballs in Marinara Sauce

Lasagna

by Jennifer Dempsey of Mother Thyme

Make tonight lasagna night with this delicious Slow Cooker Lasagna. Serve with a tossed salad and fresh garlic bread for a complete meal the entire family will love!

½ pound Italian sausage, casings removed
½ pound ground beef
½ teaspoon salt
½ teaspoon black pepper
2 jars (24 ounces each) marinara sauce
16 ounces ricotta cheese
½ cup grated Parmesan cheese
½ teaspoon dried parsley
1 cup shredded mozzarella cheese
18 lasagna noodles, broken in half or thirds
Freshly chopped basil for serving (optional)

Add Italian sausage and ground beef to a large skillet and season with salt and pepper. Cook over medium heat until cooked thoroughly. Remove from heat and stir in marinara sauce.

In a medium bowl mix ricotta cheese, Parmesan cheese, parsley, mozzarella. Season with a pinch of salt and pepper.

Pour 2 cups of the meat mixture into the slow cooker. Top with a third of the broken lasagna noodles and ½ of the ricotta mixture.

Repeat the layers one time. Top with remaining noodles and sauce (sauce should be on top).

Cook on low for about 4-5 hours. Garnish with fresh basil before serving if desired.

Serves 6   *$3.04-$3.21 per serving*

Chicken Cacciatore
by Carrie Vibert of Poet in the Pantry

An easy Italian dish perfect for any time of the year. This is delicious served over spaghetti squash, rice or egg noodles.

1 large sweet onion, sliced
6 boneless, skinless chicken thighs (roughly 1¾-2 pounds)
3 bell peppers, sliced (go for a variety of colors)
8 cloves garlic, peeled and halved
2 ounces tomato paste
2 (14½ ounce each) cans fire roasted diced tomatoes with juice
2 (14 ounce cans each) small artichoke hearts, drained
1 cup chicken broth
1 bay leaf
2 teaspoons finely chopped fresh parsley
½ teaspoon crushed red pepper
½ teaspoon dried rosemary leaves
½ teaspoon salt
¼ teaspoon freshly ground black pepper
10 fresh basil leaves, chiffonade (rolled and cut in little strips, or "ribbons")
2 ounces baby bella (cremini) mushrooms, sliced

Spread the onions over the bottom of a 6-quart slow cooker. Place the chicken on top of the onions. Top the chicken with the peppers, garlic, tomato paste, diced tomatoes, and artichoke hearts.

Pour the chicken broth over the top and add the bay leaf, parsley, crushed red pepper, rosemary, salt and pepper.

Cover and cook on low for 4 hours.

Add the basil and mushrooms and cook for an additional 10 minutes on high with the lid off. Remove bay leaf before serving.

Note: Be careful not to cook too long past 4 hours or the chicken will get overcooked and dry.

Serves 6

$4.24 per serving

Pork Tenderloin Florentine
by Carolyn Ketchum of All Day I Dream About Food

Jazz up your slow cooker pork tenderloin by rolling it and stuffing it with spinach, roasted red peppers and two cheeses. It doesn't take much extra effort and the pinwheels of pork and fillings make a lovely dinner presentation. You can also brown the tenderloin before adding it into the slow cooker, for extra flavor.

1 pork tenderloin (about 1¼ pounds)
½ cup ricotta cheese
2 cloves garlic, minced
½ teaspoon salt, plus additional to taste
¼ teaspoon pepper, plus additional to taste
½ cup chopped roasted red peppers
¼ cup crumbled feta cheese
1 cup baby spinach leaves
2 tablespoons olive oil
1 cup chicken broth
½ cup white wine

Lay the tenderloin on a cutting board and slice lengthwise about halfway through the meat, then slice from the bottom of the cut to the left side about halfway through, and to the right side about halfway through. Open the tenderloin out flat and cover with plastic wrap. Pound with a mallet to an even ½ inch thickness.

In a small bowl, mix together ricotta, garlic, salt and pepper. Spread over the flattened pork, leaving a 1 inch border. Sprinkle with roasted peppers and feta, then lay spinach leaves overtop and press down gently to adhere.

Roll the pork up from the long side and tie in several places with kitchen twine. Secure the ends with toothpicks or small skewers. Brush with olive oil and season with additional salt and pepper. If desired, brown tenderloin quickly on all sides in large skillet over medium heat.

Lay tenderloin in the bottom of the slow cooker and add broth and wine. Cook on low for 4 to 6 hours. Remove and slice into 1-inch thick slices to serve.

Serves 4

$3.57 per serving

Italian Beef Sandwiches
by Jen Nikolaus of Yummy Healthy Easy

Tender slow cooked beef that's shredded and served on buns. Flavorful and delicious with very little preparation. Serve with the juice from the meat in the slow cooker or top with barbecue sauce. A comforting dinner for a busy day!

1 onion, diced
3-4 pound boneless chuck roast
Salt and pepper
1½ packages dry Italian dressing mix
2 cloves garlic, minced
1 (14 ounce) can beef broth

Place onions in the bottom of slow cooker. Season both sides of roast with salt and pepper and place on top of onions.

Sprinkle dry Italian dressing mix over the top of the roast, then top with the minced garlic.

Pour beef broth over the meat and cook on high 4-6 hours or low for 10 hours.

When finished cooking, pull meat from slow cooker and shred with two forks. Place meat on top of buns. Serve with the juice from the meat in the slow cooker or top with barbecue sauce or ketchup. Moist and delicious!

Serves: 8   *$3.27 per serving*

Balsamic Orange Roast Beef
by Brenda Score of A Farmgirl's Dabbles

This beef comes out of the slow cooker so ultra tender that you only need a fork to dig in. It's sweet and fragrant from fresh oranges, with a lovely balsamic vinegar tang.

3½-4 pound boneless beef chuck or round roast
1 cup beef broth
½ cup balsamic vinegar
½ cup orange marmalade (I like to use a marmalade with large pieces of orange peel)
4 large cloves garlic, minced
2 tablespoons soy sauce
1 teaspoon Worcestershire sauce
¼ teaspoon red pepper flakes
Juice and zest of 1 large orange, plus orange wedges for serving
Freshly ground black pepper

Place beef roast in slow cooker. In a small bowl, whisk together beef broth, balsamic vinegar, marmalade, garlic, soy sauce, Worcestershire sauce and red pepper flakes. Pour mixture over beef, place lid on slow cooker, and cook on low heat for 6 to 8 hours, or about 4 hours on high.

Once beef is fork tender, remove it to a serving dish. Pour most of the gravy from the slow cooker (leave about ¼ cup of gravy in the slow cooker) into a medium saucepan and then return the beef to the slow cooker to keep warm. Use a fat separator to remove the obvious fat from the gravy in the saucepan. Cook gravy over medium-low to medium heat until reduced nearly by half, then stir in orange juice and zest. Remove pan from heat.

Transfer beef from slow cooker to a serving dish. Break beef apart just a bit with two forks and then pour gravy over the beef. Sprinkle with freshly ground black pepper. Serve with fresh orange wedges to squeeze over the top.

Serves 6-8   *$4.39 per serving*

Sweet Italian Sausage and Peppers
by Samantha Seeley of Sweet Remedy

A classic family recipe transformed to fit the slow cooker. Perfect on top of pasta or in a sandwich.

1 pound sweet Italian sausage
1 (16 ounce) can diced tomatoes
1 medium onion, chopped
2 red peppers, sliced
2 green peppers, sliced
1 tablespoon fresh basil, minced
3 cloves garlic, minced
1 teaspoon fresh oregano, minced
¼ teaspoon crushed red pepper
1 pound rotini pasta

In a medium skillet, cook the sausage and drain remaining grease. Once cooled, cut into 1 inch thick pieces and set aside.

In the slow cooker, layer the diced tomatoes on the bottom and top with the onions and peppers. Add garlic, basil, oregano, crushed red pepper. Stir to incorporate all ingredients.

Cook for 6 hours on low.

During the last 15 minutes of cooking, boil a large pot of water and cook the pasta according to package instructions. Drain and top with the completed sausage and peppers.

Serves 4-6 $3.93 per serving

Macaroni and Cheese with Sugar Snap Peas

by Pamela Reed of Brooklyn Farm Girl

Who doesn't love macaroni and cheese? In this recipe we mix a comfort food favorite with fresh sugar snap peas. It's the perfect combo of creamy and crunchy!

1 egg
3 cups whole milk
1 (16 ounce) box of medium shells (uncooked)
4 cups shredded cheddar cheese, divided
1 teaspoon salt
½ teaspoon ground white pepper
½ teaspoon dry mustard
2 cups sugar snap peas - cut into thirds

Lightly grease the inside of your slow cooker with oil or no-stick cooking spray.

In a bowl mix egg and milk. Pour this mixture into your slow cooker. Add uncooked shells, 3 cups of the cheddar cheese, salt, pepper and dry mustard. Mix everything together until it's combined. Sprinkle remaining 1 cup of cheese on top.

Cook on low for 2 ½ hours. Stir in the sugar snap peas and continue to cook until desired tenderness, about 30 minutes more.

Serves 4   *$3.20 per serving*

photo credit: Pamela Reed

Pork Meatballs in Marinara Sauce
by Julie Grice of Savvy Eats

Traditional meatballs and marinara get a lighter treatment when you use pork instead of beef. Serve them on their own or over pasta for a meal that the whole family will love, at any time of year.

Marinara
28 ounces crushed tomatoes
8 ounces tomato sauce
6 ounces tomato paste
2 sprigs fresh oregano (or 2 teaspoons dried oregano)
1 sprig fresh rosemary (or 1 teaspoon dried rosemary)
1 teaspoon garlic powder
1 teaspoon granulated sugar
1 teaspoon salt

Meatballs
1 pound ground pork
½ medium yellow onion, diced
2 cloves garlic, minced
⅔ cup bread crumbs
1 egg
3 tablespoons grated Parmesan cheese
1 teaspoon dried oregano
½ teaspoon salt
¼ teaspoon ground black pepper

Pour the marinara ingredients into the slow cooker and stir well to combine.

Mash all the meatball ingredients together with your hands until they form a cohesive ball. Shape the meat into 1½ inch balls, and nestle each one into the sauce, turning each meatball so that it is completely covered in sauce.

Cook on low for 4-6 hours or until meat is cooked through.

Serves 4   *$2.05 per serving*

COMFORT IN A BOWL

Chili
Butternut Squash Vegetarian Chili
Vegetarian Pumpkin White Chili
Harvest Chili

Soups
Broccoli and Cheese Potato Soup
Pumpkin, Chicken and Spinach Tortellini Soup

Stews
Cuban Seafood Stew
Lentil, Sausage and Kale Stew
Chicken, Potato and Barley Stew

Butternut Squash Vegetarian Chili

by Brandy O'Neill of Nutmeg Nanny

Don't stress out about what to make for supper. This super-simple butternut squash vegetarian chili is a great set-it-and-forget-it meal. Full of nutritious vegetables, it takes just a few hours to cook and is sure to please the whole family.

1 small yellow onion, chopped
3½ cups cubed butternut squash (½ inch cubes)
2½ cups sliced bell peppers
1 cup corn kernels
32 ounces vegetable stock
28 ounces Mexican stewed tomatoes
28 ounces canned black beans, drained and rinsed
4 ounces canned diced green chilies, drained
1 tablespoon chili powder
2 teaspoons cumin
2 teaspoons smoked paprika
1 teaspoon chipotle chile powder
Toppings (optional) - cilantro, tortilla chips, sour cream, shredded cheese

Add all ingredients (except for toppings) to a 6 quart slow cooker and heat on low for 8 hours. If liquid gets too low simply add more vegetable stock.

When you're ready to serve spoon into bowls and top with desired toppings.

Serves 6 $2.88-$3.48 per serving

Vegetarian Pumpkin White Chili
by Karen Raye of Kitchen Treaty

We are slightly obsessed over white chili in this house - and equally obsessed with pumpkin. So I thought it just might work out if I combined the two - and, yay! It does! This recipe is just perfect for fall and winter months. You can skip the sauté step and just stir it all in the slow cooker from the get-go, but I think the flavor is nicer when you cook the onion and green pepper first. To make it vegan, just omit dairy options from the topping ideas.

4 cups cooked Great Northern or cannellini beans (or 2 (15 ounces each) cans, drained)
1 tablespoon olive oil
1 medium onion, diced
1 medium green pepper, diced
3 cloves garlic, minced (about 2 teaspoons)
2 (4 ounces each) cans diced mild green chilies
2 teaspoons ground cumin
¼ teaspoon ground cloves
¼ teaspoon cayenne pepper
1 teaspoon coarse salt
1 cup puréed pumpkin (canned or fresh that has been cooked and puréed)
1 cup vegetable broth
Toppings (optional) - fresh lime wedges, cilantro, sour cream, shredded cheese, and/or tortilla chips

Add beans to slow cooker.

Place a large skillet over medium heat and add the olive oil. Sauté the onion and green pepper until softened, about 5 minutes. Add the garlic, green chiles, cumin, cloves, cayenne, and salt. Cook, stirring, for another minute. Add the pumpkin and vegetable broth and stir until combined. Pour into the slow cooker, over the beans, and stir gently to combine.

Cook on low for 8 - 10 hours, or on high 5 - 6 hours.

Taste and add additional salt and pepper if needed. Serve with toppings, if desired.

Serves 4-6 $2.02-$2.53 per serving

Harvest Chili
by Nicole Harris of Wonky Wonderful

A warm and hearty chili that is bursting with unique flavors. Perfect for enjoying on a chilly fall evening.

1 pound dried small red beans
1 pound lean ground beef
½ white onion, chopped
28 ounce canned low sodium diced tomatoes
3½ cups water
2 celery ribs, chopped
1 large sweet potato, peeled and cubed
1 orange bell pepper, seeded and chopped
1 teaspoon cumin
1 teaspoon sea salt
½ teaspoon chili powder
½ teaspoon garlic powder
½ teaspoon onion powder
¼ teaspoon ground black pepper
⅛ teaspoon ground cinnamon
Pinch of cayenne pepper (optional)

Rinse and sort beans. Soak in 6-8 cups cold water overnight. Drain and rinse.

Brown ground beef and onions on stove top over medium heat. Drain fat.

Combine beans, browned ground beef and all other ingredients in a large slow cooker. Cover and slow cook for 4-5 hours on high or 7-8 hours on low.

Serves 8   *$1.63 per serving*

Broccoli and Cheese Potato Soup
by Angela Barrett of Big Bear's Wife

This broccoli and cheese soup is loaded with hearty red potatoes and packed full of wonderful vegetables. It's the perfect way to warm up in the evenings!

2 pounds red potatoes, cubed
2 tablespoons butter
2 cups chicken broth
8 ounces mushrooms, chopped
1 carrot, grated
½ pound broccoli, chopped
6 cups whole milk
2 cups heavy cream (or half and half)
16 ounces grated cheddar cheese
2 cloves garlic, minced
Salt and pepper to taste

Turn the slow cooker onto low. Add the red potatoes and butter to the bowl of the slow cooker. Pour in the chicken broth. Stir in the mushrooms, grated carrot and broccoli.

Pour in the milk and heavy cream. Stir to combine. Stir in the cheese and minced garlic. Cover and cook the soup on low for 8 hours or until potatoes are very tender; season with salt and pepper to taste.

Tip for a smoother soup: After cooking, remove a few cups of soup and carefully purée in a blender. Add the puréed soup back to the slow cooker and stir to combine.

Serves 8-10

$2.17 per serving

Pumpkin, Chicken and Spinach Tortellini Soup

by Faith Gorsky of An Edible Mosaic

Pumpkin, sage, a hint of brown sugar and a touch of nutmeg give this dish a subtle, but distinctive fall feel. Somewhere between the consistency of stew and a bowl of pasta with sauce, this hearty soup is perfect fare for a chilly evening.

2 tablespoons olive oil
1 pound chicken breast, trimmed of fat and cubed
1 large onion, diced
3 large cloves garlic, crushed
3-4 cups low-sodium chicken stock
15 ounce can pumpkin purée (not pumpkin pie mix)
2 teaspoons brown sugar
1½ teaspoons minced fresh sage leaves (or ½ teaspoon dried crushed sage leaves or ¼ teaspoon dried powdered sage)
1 teaspoon salt
¼ teaspoon freshly ground black pepper
⅛ teaspoon freshly ground nutmeg
1 bay leaf
9 ounce package fresh cheese tortellini
4 cups fresh baby spinach leaves, washed
1 tablespoon fresh lemon juice

Preheat slow cooker on low setting.

Heat the oil in a large skillet over medium-high to high heat. Once hot, add the chicken and cook until browned outside, about 4 minutes. (Wait to stir the chicken until after it's brown on the first side.) Add the onion and cook for 3 minutes, stirring occasionally. Add the garlic and cook for 1 minute, stirring constantly.

Transfer the chicken mixture to the preheated slow cooker and stir in 3 cups of chicken stock, the pumpkin purée, brown sugar, salt, black pepper, nutmeg, bay leaf, and sage. Cover and cook for 3 hours on low.

Add the tortellini and cook until tender, about 1 hour on low. (You can add up to 1 more cup of chicken stock to thin it out if you want, depending on how much liquid the pasta absorbs.)

Stir in the spinach leaves, and then cover the pot and let them wilt, about 1 minute. Stir in the fresh lemon juice. Serve.

Serves 4-6 $3.94 per serving

Cuban Seafood Stew
by Dianna Muscari of The Kitchen Prep

This simple dish is packed with flavor, but doesn't take much time at all to throw together. The flavors of bay leaves, green peppers, onion and garlic infuse the broth that gently cooks the shrimp and flaky cod. Served over rice, it's like a big, warm hug from a Cuban grandma.

1 tablespoon olive oil
1 large onion, diced
1 large green pepper, seeded and diced
3 cloves garlic, grated or finely minced
½ teaspoon ground cumin
½ teaspoon dried oregano
½ teaspoon sea salt
2 bay leaves
3 medium Roma or plum tomatoes, diced
12-15 small new potatoes, quartered
2 tablespoons tomato paste
2½ cups chicken broth or fish stock
1 pound cod -- 2 half pound filets, cut in half
½ pound shrimp, peeled and deveined
Toppings (optional) - lime wedges, cilantro

In a large sauté pan, heat the olive oil over medium-high heat. Add onion to the pan and cook for about 3-4 minutes. Add green pepper and continue to cook another 4-5 minutes, until vegetables are softened and slightly golden.

Stir in garlic, cumin, oregano and salt and cook for another 1-2 minutes. Transfer mixture to slow cooker insert.

Toss in bay leaves, tomatoes, potatoes and tomato paste. Gently mix the ingredients together until well combined. Pour in chicken broth or fish stock and stir gently. Cover and cook on high for about 3 hours.

Add fish and shrimp to the mixture, making sure to submerge under liquid, and cook for another 30 minutes or until the fish flakes easily with a fork and the shrimp is pink and opaque.

Garnish with cilantro and lime wedges if desired.

Serves 4   *$6.67-$6.85 per serving*

Lentil, Sausage and Kale Stew
by Jeanette Chen of Jeanette's Healthy Living

This hearty stew is perfect for a cool fall day or in the thick of winter. Try different varieties of chicken sausage to mix things up.

4 cups low sodium chicken broth
3 cooked chicken Italian sausages, cut into bite-size pieces
1 cup dried lentils
1 onion, chopped
2 carrots, chopped
1 celery rib, chopped
2 cloves garlic, minced
2 teaspoons Herbs de Provence or your favorite herb blend
2 cups kale, chopped

Place broth, sausage, lentils, onion, carrots, celery, garlic and Herbs de Provence in slow cooker. Cover and cook on low for 8 hours.

Season to taste with salt and pepper and add kale. Cover and cook 15 minutes more.

Serves 6   *$1.41 per serving*

Chicken, Potato and Barley Stew
by Renee Dobbs of Magnolia Days

A hearty and comforting stew filled with tender chicken, vegetables, barley, and beans. It is a delicious, healthy and satisfying meal for your family.

32 ounces low-sodium chicken broth
1 medium carrot, peeled and cut into ¼ inch pieces
1 celery rib, cut into ¼ inch pieces
1 medium russet potato, peeled and cut into bite-sized pieces
1 medium onion, chopped
½ cup uncooked pearled barley
½ cup dried navy beans (or your favorite dried bean)
½ teaspoon salt
¼ teaspoon ground black pepper
1½ pounds skinless chicken legs

Add the chicken broth, carrot, celery, potato, onion, barley, beans, salt, and pepper to a 3½ to 6-quart slow cooker. Stir ingredients.

Add the chicken legs and push them down into the mixture.

Cover and cook 5 to 6 hours on low or 3 to 4 hours on high, until the chicken is cooked through and the barley and beans are tender.

Transfer chicken legs to a plate. Remove the meat and use a fork to pull apart into smaller pieces. Add the chicken pieces back to the stew and stir to combine. Discard the bones and cartilage. Serve immediately.

Serves 4   *$1.97 per serving*

FOOD FOR A FIESTA

Tex-Mex Scalloped Potato and Carrot Dinner
Barbacoa Tacos
Chicken Burritos Bowls
Raspberry-Chipotle Chicken Tacos
Sweet and Spicy Carnitas
Cuban Black Bean Soup
Strawberry-Habanero Pulled Chicken

Tex-Mex Scalloped Potato and Carrot Dinner
by Christine Pittman of Cook the Story

I love to give scalloped potatoes a twist by adding other ingredients. One time I went with Tex-Mex flavors like chili powder, tomatoes, corn and cheddar. My family liked it so much that I decided to turn it into a complete dinner by adding ground beef for protein and carrots for a larger healthy vegetable portion.

1½ pound ground beef
1½ teaspoon salt, divided
1 (28 ounce) can low-sodium crushed tomatoes
1 (28 ounce) can low-sodium diced tomatoes, drained
1 (15 ounce) can low-sodium black beans, drained and rinsed
1 green bell pepper, seeded and chopped
1 tablespoon chili powder
1 teaspoon garlic powder
¼ teaspoon black pepper
2½ pounds russet potatoes, in ¼ inch slices
1 (16 ounce) bag crinkle-cut carrot chips
12 ounces cheddar cheese, shredded
2 spring onions, chopped

Heat a large skillet over medium-high heat. Add the ground beef and ½ teaspoon of the salt. Cook, stirring occasionally, until cooked through, 4-6 minutes. Drain off any fat or juices. Transfer beef to a large bowl along with the remaining 1 teaspoon of salt, crushed tomatoes, diced tomatoes, black beans, bell pepper, chili powder, garlic powder and black pepper. Stir well. Taste and add more salt and pepper if desired.

Measure 1 cup of the beef and sauce mixture into a 6 quart slow cooker. Put one quarter of the potatoes in a single over-lapping layer over the sauce. Add a carrot chip in between each slice of potato. Top with 2 cups sauce and then ½ cup of cheese.

Add a second layer of potatoes and carrots, 2 cups more sauce and ¾ cup of cheese. Repeat until you have 4 layers of potatoes total, finishing off by using all remaining sauce and cheese in the final layer.

Cook in the slow cooker on high for 4 hours. Open lid and spoon off any liquid that has risen to the top and discard it (this top liquid contains excessive grease from the cheese and meat). Let sit with the lid open for 15 minutes. Use a slotted spoon to serve. Top servings with the spring onions.

Serves 6-8

$3.49 per serving

Barbacoa Tacos
by Jessica Reddick Gatlin of My Baking Heart

Spicy and just perfect for warming up on chilly nights. This Barbacoa Beef is easy to prepare and can be enjoyed in several different dishes, not just as tacos. It's a staple for us, whether we're tailgating at TCU football games or sitting next to the fire on a Sunday evening.

2 tablespoons chili powder
3 teaspoons ground cumin
2 teaspoons garlic powder
2 teaspoons kosher salt
2 teaspoons black pepper
1 teaspoon dried oregano
1 teaspoon paprika
½ teaspoon crushed red pepper flakes
3½ pounds beef chuck roast
¾ cup beef stock
2 cups salsa verde, divided
½ white onion, roughly chopped
Flour tortillas
Toppings (optional) - pico de gallo, fresh cilantro, shredded cheese

In a small bowl whisk together chili powder, cumin, garlic powder, salt, pepper, oregano, paprika and red pepper flakes. Trim any excess fat off the roast, then rub with the seasoning mix.

Place the roast in a slow cooker and pour the beef stock, then 1 cup of salsa verde, over the meat. Scatter the onions around the roast. Cook on high for 6 hours or on low for 8 hours.

When the roast is fully cooked, remove the meat from the cooker and drain the juices. Shred the meat, replacing it in the cooker, then top with the remaining cup of salsa verde, stirring to coat. Serve on tortillas with some of the optional toppings, if desired.

Serves 6-8

$4.48-$5.41 per serving

Chicken Burrito Bowls

by Gretchen Fritsch and Shelley Fulton of Two Healthy Kitchens

So easy and incredibly delicious! It only takes a few minutes to start this recipe in your slow cooker, but it's a huge hit for family dinners and casual potlucks. Bursting with flavor and full of nutritious ingredients, this will become your new Mexican night favorite!

1½ pounds boneless, skinless chicken breasts
1.25 ounce packet low-sodium taco seasoning
1½ cups fresh or frozen corn kernels (from about two ears of corn if using fresh)
1 (15 ounce) can black beans, drained and rinsed (preferably organic or reduced-sodium)
½ cup finely chopped onions
1 (16 ounce) jar of your favorite salsa
1 (10 ounce) can diced tomatoes and green chiles with juice (such as Ro-Tel)
½ cup finely chopped cilantro
Brown rice, cooked and hot, for serving
Toppings (optional) - shredded lettuce, chopped tomatoes, shredded reduced-fat cheese, chopped avocados or guacamole, reduced-fat sour cream, chopped green onions, additional chopped fresh cilantro, and hot sauce.

Place chicken in the slow cooker. Sprinkle taco seasoning, corn, black beans, and onions over chicken. Pour salsa and canned tomatoes on top. Cook on high for 4 hours or on low for 6-8 hours.

Just before serving, use two forks to shred the chicken. Add cilantro. Stir to combine ingredients.

Serve over brown rice with some of the optional toppings, if desired.

Serves 6-8 $2.76-$3.79 per serving

photo credit: Gretchen Fritsch and Shelley Fulton

Raspberry-Chipotle Chicken Tacos
by Nicole White of The Marvelous Misadventures of a Foodie

These raspberry chipotle chicken tacos are a fun way to switch up you weekly taco night. The warm and smoky heat from the chipotle pairs perfectly with the sweetness of the raspberry - it will have you coming back for more! We like to top our tacos with come fresh cilantro and some Mexican cotija cheese, but any of your favorite taco toppings will taste great.

2 pounds boneless, skinless chicken breasts, cut in half
⅓ cup plus 2 tablespoons raspberry preserves or seedless raspberry jam, divided
2 chipotle peppers in adobo sauce
1 clove garlic
1 tablespoon adobo sauce (from canned chipotle peppers)
1 tablespoon kosher salt
½ teaspoon cumin
1 (15 ounce) can diced fire roasted tomatoes
Salt and pepper
Tortillas
Toppings (optional) - cotija cheese, cilantro, avocado, sour cream, etc.

Place chicken breasts in a single layer in the bottom of the slow cooker.

In a food processor combine ⅓ cup raspberry jam, chipotle peppers, garlic, adobo sauce, salt and cumin, Purée until mixture is smooth.

Pour chipotle mixture over the chicken breast then cover with the fire roasted tomatoes. Gently lift chicken to allow some of the tomatoes and juice to get underneath. Cook on low for 5-6 hours, or on high for 2-4 hours.

Shred the chicken with some or all of the cooking liquid. Stir in remaining 2 tablespoons of raspberry jam, then season with salt and pepper to taste.

To serve, place chicken onto tortillas and top with desired taco toppings.

Note: You can find canned chipotle peppers in adobo sauce in the Latin aisle of most grocery stores.

Serves 6-8

$2.44-$3.04 per serving

Sweet and Spicy Carnitas
by Kim Beaulieu of Cravings of a Lunatic and Kiss My Smoke

My family loves pulled pork. This Carnita recipe is always a hit in our household. It combines the perfect amount of heat with a just a hint of sweet. Scoop it into tacos with all your favorite toppings. Taco night has never been easier.

3 ½ pounds boneless pork shoulder roast, such as pork butt or blade
2 teaspoons brown sugar
1 teaspoon ancho chile pepper
1 teaspoon smoked paprika
1 teaspoon coarse salt
1 teaspoon white pepper
1 teaspoon dried cilantro
½ teaspoon cumin
½ teaspoon coriander
½ teaspoon red pepper flakes
8 ounces Coke (use water if watching your sugar consumption)
8 ounces water
2 oranges
2 limes
3 cloves garlic
Toppings (optional) -1 package of corn or flour tortillas, 1-2 tomatoes (cut into small chunks), 1/2 red onion (diced), 1/2 bunch of green onions (diced), an avocado (sliced thinly), fresh cilantro leaves, salsa, lettuce (shredded)

Remove pork shoulder from fridge. Set aside. In a medium sized bowl combine the brown sugar, ancho chile pepper, smoked paprika, coarse salt, white pepper, dried cilantro, cumin, coriander and red pepper flakes. Mix well so all the spices combine thoroughly. Carefully rub the entire pork roast with the spice rub, making sure to coat all the sides. Place the pork shoulder in you slow cooker. Pour the Coke and water around the side of the roast, but not over top of it. Cut the oranges in half, squeeze the juice out over the roast. Place the pieces inside the slow cooker. Cut the limes in half, squeeze the juice out over the roast. Place the pieces inside the slow cooker. Place the garlic cloves in the liquid as well. Cover and cook for 9 to 10 hours, you want the meat to be moist, and to pull apart easily.

Transfer the meat to a cutting board and pull it apart with two forks. Place the meat in a large frying pan with a touch of olive oil. Cook over medium-high heat for about 3 to 5 minutes. I find adding just a touch of brown sugar helps to caramelize quickly. The key to great carnitas is having the meat be moist but the edges crispy. Remove from heat and transfer to a large bowl.

Meanwhile, prepare any optional toppings you plan to serve, except for the avocado. Do that at the last minute so it doesn't brown before serving. Shortly before the pork is done, heat the tortillas by placing them in a frying pan, one at a time, flipping so you warm each side. Alternately you can warm them in the microwave all at once for about 30 to 45 seconds. Keep warm until serving. Top each tortilla with meat and toppings of your choice. Serve with a big old sweet and spicy smile!

Serves 4-6

$2.89-$3.94 *per serving*

Cuban Black Bean Soup
by April Aceto of Food n' Focus

Putting a twist on a classic fall soup, this Cuban infused slow cooker meal delivers intense flavors with a bit of spice. Topping off the soup with cool sour cream and garnishes completes the meal.

2 tablespoons extra virgin olive oil
1 large white onion, finely chopped
1 red bell pepper, finely chopped
6 cloves garlic, finely chopped
1 bay leaf
2 teaspoons cumin
1 teaspoon oregano
1 teaspoon black pepper
7 cups water
1 pound dried black beans, rinsed thoroughly, soaked overnight
1 cup pulp-free orange juice
1 medium orange, zested
2 tablespoons sherry vinegar
½ cup dry white wine
2 teaspoons salt
Toppings (optional) - tomato, red onion, jalapeno, sour cream

Heat the oil in a large pan. Add the onion, pepper and garlic and sauté for 2-3 minutes. Add the bay leaf, cumin, oregano and black pepper and cook for an additional 2 minutes.

Place the sautéed mixture into the slow cooker along with the water, soaked beans, orange juice and zest. Stir gently to combine. Cook on low for 6 hours.

Add the vinegar, wine and salt and continue to cook for 1 additional hour. Remove the bay leaf before serving garnished with optional toppings, if desired.

Serves 8   *$1.06-$1.32 per serving*

Strawberry-Habanero Pulled Chicken

by Lauren Keating of Healthy. Delicious.

The sweet heat of habanero peppers combined with puréed strawberries make a flavorful sauce for this pulled chicken. Top the chicken with creamy avocado slices and serve it piled high on whole wheat rolls. Don't let the habanero pepper scare you away – the long slow cooking tames its heat and brings out its natural sweetness.

1 cup fresh or frozen strawberry purée
¼ small onion, minced
2 cloves garlic, smashed
1 habanero pepper, minced
1 tablespoon honey
1 tablespoon apple cider vinegar
1 tablespoon molasses
1 teaspoon tomato paste
½ teaspoon liquid smoke
1 pinch salt
1 pound boneless, skinless chicken breasts
4 sandwich rolls, preferably whole wheat
1 avocado, sliced (optional)

Combine first ten ingredients (through the salt) in your slow cooker. Mix well. Add the chicken breasts, turning so they are coated with the sauce.

Cover and cook on high for 4 hours. Use the back of a wooden spoon to gently shred the chicken. Stir so that the shredded chicken is evenly coated with the sauce. Set slow cooker to warm and let chicken stand for 15 minutes to soak up the sauce.

Serve the pulled chicken on rolls. Top with avocado slices, if desired.

Serves 4 $2.28–$2.85 per serving

TAKE OUT NIGHT

Chicken Korma
Chinese Beef and Broccoli
Island Jerk Pulled Pork
Thai Pork with Vermicelli Salad
Spiced Lentil Stew
Thai Coconut Curry Beef and Broccoli

Chicken Korma

Christine Pittman of Cook the Story

Chicken Korma is a creamy chicken dish that is a staple on Indian restaurant menus. For this easy slow cooker version, chicken and spices cook together for hours. You then add some yogurt at the end for a bit of healthy creaminess. It's lovely served with brown basmati rice or a flatbread like naan or pita.

5 medium tomatoes (about 1½ pounds), seeded and chopped
2 medium onions, chopped
3 cloves garlic, minced
1 tablespoon grated fresh ginger
2 teaspoons curry powder
2 teaspoons garam masala
½ teaspoon salt
¼ teaspoon red pepper flakes
8 skinless chicken drumsticks
½ cup plain yogurt or plain Greek yogurt
¼ cup chopped fresh cilantro

Into a slow cooker put the tomatoes, onions, garlic, ginger, curry powder, garam masala, salt and red pepper flakes. Stir. Add the chicken. Use your hands to really mix it around so that the chicken meat is coated in the tomato and spice mixture.

Cook until chicken is cooked through and is very tender, 3-4 hours on high, 6-7 hours on low.

Remove chicken drumsticks from slow cooker. Separate meat and bones. Return the meat to the slow cooker. Stir in the yogurt. Season to taste with salt. Serve garnished with cilantro.

Serves 4 $3.35 per serving

Chinese Beef and Broccoli
by Amy Flanigan of Very Culinary

This classic Chinese take-out favorite just got even easier. Make it right in your slow cooker! A flavorful and rich sauce coats tender sirloin and colorful broccoli. A complete meal the entire family will love.

¼ cup low sodium soy sauce
¼ cup oyster sauce
2 tablespoons rice wine vinegar
2 teaspoons vegetable oil
2 teaspoons plus ¼ teaspoon sugar, divided
¼ teaspoon white pepper
4 cloves garlic, minced
1 tablespoon minced ginger
1 tablespoon cornstarch
¼ teaspoon baking soda
¼ teaspoon salt
2 tablespoons water
1 pound beef sirloin, cut into 1-inch pieces
1 medium sweet onion, cut into 1-inch pieces
1 large head of broccoli, cut up into florets, steamed until tender
Cooked white rice for serving

Lightly grease the inside of your slow cooker with oil or no-stick cooking spray.

In a small bowl, whisk together the soy sauce, oyster sauce, vinegar, vegetable oil, 2 teaspoons of the sugar, pepper, garlic, and ginger until combined.

In a medium bowl, stir together the cornstarch, baking soda, salt, remaining ¼ teaspoon sugar, and water. Add the sirloin and mix until well coated.

Shake off any excess powder from the meat and place in the slow cooker, along with the onions and sauce mixture.

Cook on low for 4 hours. Gently stir in the broccoli and mix to combine with the sauce. Serve over cooked white rice.

Note: If you'd like your meat to have a somewhat dark crispy exterior, cook in a nonstick pan with a bit of oil over high heat for one minute, without stirring, before placing it in the slow cooker.

Serves 4-6 $2.90 per serving

Island Jerk Pulled Pork

by Jill Holland, Sous Chef of Catering for Good and Chef Instructor of Second Harvest Food Bank of Central Florida

Get all the warm spicy jerk flavors in an easy-to-make pulled pork sandwich.

1 tablespoon onion powder
1 tablespoon garlic powder
2 teaspoons grated fresh ginger
1½ teaspoons ground cloves
1½ teaspoons ground allspice
1½ teaspoons thyme
1½ teaspoons dry mustard
1½ teaspoons coarse salt
1 teaspoon sweet or hot paprika
½ teaspoon cumin
½ teaspoon sugar
¼ teaspoon black pepper
¼ teaspoon cayenne pepper
3 pound boneless pork butt
1 cup apple cider or apple juice
1 bay leaf
8-10 hamburger buns, sliced open
Toppings (optional) - BBQ sauce, fresh cilantro

In a small bowl combine onion powder, garlic powder, ginger, cloves, allspice, thyme, dry mustard, salt, paprika, cumin, sugar, black pepper and cayenne. Use fingers to rub spices together to ensure that ginger is dispersed throughout. Rub spice mixture all over pork.

Put the pork in the slow cooker fat side up. Pour apple cider over pork and add bay leaf. Cook on low for 8 hours.

Remove pork from slow cooker. Use two forks to shred meat. Skim fat off liquid in slow cooker. Drizzle a few tablespoons of the remaining liquid over the meat and mix to combine.

Serve on a bun as-is or slathered with your favorite BBQ sauce and sprinkled with fresh cilantro.

Serves 8-10 $2.29-$3.29 *per serving*

photo credit: Christine Pittman

Thai Pork with Vermicelli Salad
by Jane Craske of Jane's Adventures in Dinner

Our family loves the taste of Thai food, but getting to it is often a challenge. How about Thai food that is ready the moment that you walk in the door and costs a fraction of what a restaurant dinner would run you?

2 dried chilies
2 tablespoons fish sauce
3 tablespoon red Thai curry paste
8 ounces coconut milk
2 tablespoons lemon grass paste
2 teaspoons raw sugar
3 shallots, halved
1 yellow pepper, chopped
1 red pepper, chopped
2 teaspoons cumin
2 tablespoons soy sauce
1½ cups chopped fresh mango
2 tablespoons chopped ginger
3 cloves garlic, chopped
2 tablespoons sweet chili sauce
½ cup water
1 pound cubed pork (loin or chops work very well)

For the salad
¼ cup each chopped mint and cilantro
½ cup toasted slivered almonds
1 cup chopped red pepper
1 large carrot (grated, julienned or spiraled)
½ package of reconstituted vermicelli noodles

Add the chilies, fish sauce, curry paste, coconut milk, lemon grass, sugar, shallots, half of the yellow pepper, half of the red pepper, cumin, soy sauce, mango, ginger, garlic, chili sauce, water and pork into the slow cooker.

Cover and cook on high for 4 hours or on low for 6-8 hours. Add the other half of the yellow and red bell peppers and cook for another 30 minutes.

Mix salad ingredients together. Place a portion of the salad on a plate and top with pork, peppers and a bit of the sauce.

Serves 6   *$3.95 per serving*

Spiced Lentil Stew

by Lisa Le of Je suis alimentageuse

This Spiced Lentil Stew is great for a light yet filling meal full of protein, fiber, iron, and warm spiced comfort. You can adjust it to make it spicier (adding more chili flakes and black pepper) or sweeter (more molasses). This stew is best made with a flavorful vegetable broth with lots of sweet onions and carrots and umami mushroom flavors.

1 medium onion, diced
¾ cup dry green lentils, rinsed and picked through
½ cup dry split red lentils, rinsed and picked through
1 teaspoon molasses
2 tablespoons olive oil
1 teaspoon black pepper
1 teaspoon garlic powder
1 teaspoon turmeric
½ teaspoon cumin
¼ teaspoon cinnamon
1 pinch chili flakes
5 cups vegetable broth
1½ teaspoon salt (to taste)
Toppings (optional) - lime juice, cilantro

In a small saucepan over medium heat, dry cook the onions until translucent and lightly browned. Transfer to slow cooker pot. Add both types of lentils and molasses.

In the same small saucepan, bloom oil and spices by heating up the oil, black pepper, garlic powder, turmeric, cumin, cinnamon, chili flakes over low heat, stirring until fragrant.

Pour over lentils. Add the vegetable broth. Cover and let cook on low for 6-8 hours, or high for 2-3 hours.

Add salt to taste (do not add salt until after the lentils are cooked as salt tends to prevent lentils from becoming tender during the cooking process).

Serve with a splash of lime juice and sprinkle of cilantro over the stew, if desired.

Serves 2-4   *$2.86 per serving*

photo credit: Lisa Le

Thai Coconut Curry Beef and Broccoli
by Taylor Kiser of Food Faith Fitness

A Thai twist on the classic take-out dish. It's perfect for a cold, winter evening when you need a little kick to warm you up!

1½ cups reduced-fat coconut milk
3 tablespoons yellow curry powder
1½ tablespoons packed brown sugar
2½ teaspoons fish sauce
½ tablespoon minced garlic
1 teaspoon minced ginger
¼ teaspoon red pepper flakes
1 pound beef chuck roast, fat removed, cut into thin strips
1 tablespoon cornstarch
1 pound broccoli florets
Hot cooked brown rice or quinoa for serving

In the slow cooker whisk together the coconut milk, curry powder, brown sugar, fish sauce, garlic, ginger and red pepper flakes. Add the beef strips and toss to coat. Cover and cook on low heat for 4-6 hours, until the meat is tender. Mine was perfect at 4 hours.

In a small bowl combine 2 tablespoons of the liquid from the slow cooker with the cornstarch. Whisk until smooth. Stir into the slow cooker and add the broccoli. Cook an additional 30 minutes to an hour, until the sauce slightly thickens.

Serve over brown rice or quinoa.

Serves 4   *$3.61 per serving*

Acknowledgments

The idea for this book came about because we were pushed together at an event where we subsequently became better friends, realized how complementary we are to each other and decided we absolutely had to work together. We are grateful to that event.

We are also grateful to the amazing bloggers who agreed to join us on this project. Their recipes and photography are more beautiful than we ever imagined. We had given them specifications for the food styling and photography, which they followed enthusiastically. The result is a seamless book that flows and goes together, representing us as a group of talented women who care about others and can get things done. Are we ever grateful to be part of that group! And to know each and every one of them, either in person or online, because they inspire us every day.

A big thank you to Maria and Sacha at the Second Harvest Food Bank of Central Florida. We approached them with the idea for this book and they immediately jumped on board and threw so many ideas our way. We are especially grateful to Jill Holland, the Chef Instructor from the food bank, for contributing a recipe. It means a lot to us to have the food bank represented so strongly within the pages of this book.

To help make the launch of this book successful, to make sure that it generates donations to the Second Harvest Food Bank of Central Florida and that it works as an incentive for food banks across the country, we reached out to some sponsors for support. These sponsors have helped out in numerous ways by supplying us with items to give away on our blogs as part of the launch, by publicizing the book and by pledging money to their local food banks as part of their help to the project. We are so very grateful to the following sponsors: Hamilton Beach, San Miguel Produce, Grimmway Farms and Old Oak Farms by RPE Produce.

Thank you to Melinda, Heidi and their team at FullTilt Marketing for believing in us for this project and for so many others. And for their help contacting and coordinating sponsors, food banks, media and so much more. Their friendship and their constant effectiveness are beyond value to us.

Finally we need to thank our favorite taste-testers, our families. They ate a lot of slow cooked food and supported us through many a late night (and several grumpy early mornings) to get this book together. We don't know what we would do without your love, support and especially without all of your hugs, smiles and giggles. We love you guys. xoxo

From Jennifer and Christine

Index

INDEX

Made in the USA
Lexington, KY
06 November 2014